SCIENCE SQUAD

Written by Lisa Burke
Consultant Professor Robert Winston

Penguin Random House

Senior editor Sam Priddy
Senior art editor Fiona Macdonald
Designer and illustrator Bettina Myklebust Stovne
Additional editing Jolyon Goddard, Katy Lennon, Megan Weal, Amina Youssef
Managing editor Laura Gilbert
Managing art editor Diane Peyton Jones
DTP designer Rajesh Singh
Jacket designer Elle Ward
Producer, Pre-Production Rebecca Fallowfield
Producer Isabell Schart
Creative director Helen Senior
Publishing director Sarah Larter

Educational consultants Jacqueline Harris, Trent Kirkpatrick

First published in Great Britain in 2018 by
Dorling Kindersley Limited
80 Strand, London, WC2R 0RL

A CIP catalogue record for this book is available from the British Library.
ISBN: 978-0-2413-0185-2

Printed and bound in China

A WORLD OF IDEAS:
SEE ALL THERE IS TO KNOW

www.dk.com

Contents

Introduction

This book is about science and how it's used. Science is about trying to understand our surroundings – the world and Universe around us and all the things and creatures in it, from atoms to huge mountains, from tiny bacteria to large whales. As we learn more, we find so much that is puzzling. What lies outside the Universe we can see with a telescope, and how does the brain think and feel love?

It is important to know as much about science as we can so that we use our inventions, our technology, wisely. They can be used for the good of everybody, but science used in the wrong way can be harmful. You are fortunate because we now know so much more than when I was a child, and books like this did not exist. Properly used, the knowledge that science brings helps us to be healthier and to live better lives.

Robert Winston.

Professor Robert Winston

Meet the
Science Squad

The Science Squad is made up of different subjects that work together to show you how the world works.

Science

is all about asking questions and discovering the answers to explain how things work.

Technology

uses science to create new machines and more effective ways of doing things.

Engineering

is all about finding and designing solutions to problems – using science, technology, and maths.

Art

is all about using your imagination and style to create brilliant new things.

Maths

is about numbers, patterns, and problem-solving.

We'll be here to help you with handy tips!

The Universe

The Universe is everything around us. Some of this we can see, but most we cannot. It is a huge expanse of mainly empty space, with billions of galaxies, each containing millions of stars.

The Big Bang

Astronomers believe the Universe exploded out of a tiny point about 14 billion years ago. This is known as the Big Bang. Before this, the Universe did not exist. It is still continuing to expand today.

Light travels really fast, but space is so enormous that it takes time to reach us. This means that when we look into the Universe, we are only ever viewing the past! Light travels nearly 10 trillion km (6 million miles) a year. Scientists call this a light year, and use it to measure the huge distances in space.

There are more stars in the Universe than grains of sand on all of the beaches on Earth.

The Hubble Telescope travels 600 km (370 miles) above the Earth. It took this photo of the Universe!
Astronomers are scientists who study space.
It can get really cold in space because the stars and galaxies are so spread out.
Our Solar System was formed billions of years after the Big Bang.

The Solar System

The Solar System is made up of our nearest star, the Sun, and everything that orbits, or travels around, it. This include planets, moons, comets, asteroids, smaller rocks, and dust.

Sun

The Sun is a kind of star that scientists call a yellow dwarf.

Our star

The Sun is a medium-sized star. The Sun's powerful force of gravity pulls on the planets, keeping them in orbit around it.

Mercury is the smallest planet in the Solar System. It's a little bigger than our Moon.

People have invented ways to study and travel around our Solar System.

Earth

Earth is the only planet that we know for sure has life on it.

Mercury

Venus

Mars

Mars is known as the "Red Planet" as its dusty surface contains rust.

Asteroid belt

Scientists think the asteroid belt contains the leftover rocks from when the planets were formed.

Venus has thousands of volcanoes on its surface.

Many spacecraft have visited Mars to study its weather, surface, and rocks.

If it was possible, it would take a jumbo jet about 400 years to fly from Earth to Neptune.

The Kuiper belt is a very distant part of the Solar System. It is the home of icy dwarf planets and comets.

Kuiper belt

Pluto

Neptune

Neptune is the furthest planet from the Sun, which makes it freezing cold!

Pluto is the largest dwarf planet in the Kuiper belt.

Saturn

Saturn has more than 50 moons. It is most famous for its rings, which are made of lumps of ice and rock.

Unlike the other planets, Uranus spins on its side. This might have been caused by a collision with an Earth-sized object.

Uranus

Launched in 1977, the space probe Voyager 2 reached Neptune in 1989.

Milky Way

Our Solar System is part of a galaxy called the Milky Way. It is spiral in shape and has more than 100 billion stars. Scientists think there is a huge black hole, sucking in dust, gas, and light, at its centre.

Jupiter is by far the largest planet in our Solar System. It is made mostly of gas and has more than 60 moons orbiting it.

Jupiter

Jupiter is so huge that all the other planets in the Solar System could fit inside it.

You are here!

Solar flares
Gigantic explosions on the Sun's surface blast energy outwards. These are called solar flares.

Sunspots
Dark, cooler patches that develop on the Sun's surface are known as sunspots. They often appear in pairs and last a few weeks.

The surface of the Sun is a sizzling hot 6,000°C (11,000°F). That's 30 times hotter than an oven!

At the Sun's core, temperatures soar to around 15 million °C (27 million °F)!

Our super Sun

The Sun is our nearest star and it sits at the centre of our Solar System. It is a massive ball of burning gases, mostly hydrogen and helium, which produces an enormous amount of energy.

Total solar eclipse

A total solar eclipse occurs when the Moon passes in front of the Sun and covers its face perfectly. This blocks out most of the light, making it appear as if it is night-time.

Solar prominences
Huge eruptions from the Sun's surface are called solar prominences. They form loops due to the Sun's invisible magnetic field.

Some sunshine is good for us. We need it to make vitamin D, which helps our bones stay healthy.

8 minutes

It takes eight minutes for the Sun's light to reach Earth.

Solar panels

Lightning speed

Light travels really fast, but it still takes time to get to us on Earth. A light year is the distance a beam of light would travel in one year.

Life on Earth

Animals and plants depend on energy from the Sun to survive. Technology, such as solar panels, has been developed to absorb the Sun's energy and turn it into electricity.

The Earth

Earth is our home and the only planet known to contain life. It is just the right distance from the Sun for plants and animals to survive.

Sun rays

The middle of the planet, the equator, gets a fairly constant amount of direct sunshine.

> Summer happens in the northern half of the world when that part is tilted towards the Sun.

> Countries near the equator have a wet and a dry season, rather than spring, summer, autumn, and winter.

Seasons

We have different seasons on Earth because the planet is slightly tilted. This means that at different times of the year different parts of the planet are closer to the Sun.

> Earth's axis is tilted at an angle of 23.5°.

Land takes up about one-third of the Earth's surface.

Crust

Upper Mantle

Lower Mantle

Outer Core

Inner Core

Inside the Earth

The Earth is made many different layers, a bit like an onion. The rocky outer layer is the crust. The upper and lower mantles consist of hot rock, while the outer and inner cores are hot metal.

It is colder in the winter because the sunlight is weaker.

Stardust

Everything on Earth is made from materials that were created when dying stars exploded. Even you are made of stardust!

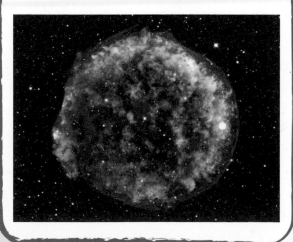

Oceans make up most of the Earth's surface, so our planet looks blue from space.

The Earth spins around an imaginary line through its middle, called an axis, once a day. This is why we have day and night.

The Earth's atmosphere

The atmosphere is a blanket of gases that surrounds and protects the Earth. It keeps us warm, blocks some of the Sun's harmful rays, and helps stop space rocks from hitting us.

Auroras

These dazzling coloured lights dance in the night sky in places close to the North and South Poles. They are also called the northern and southern lights.

Auroras happen when tiny particles from the Sun hit particles in our atmosphere.

Meteorites

Space rocks that make it through our atmosphere and hit the ground without burning up are called meteorites.

Weather balloon

Launched every day, weather balloons help forecasters predict the weather. The balloons carry small tools to measure things, such as air temperature and wind speed.

Aeroplanes

Planes usually cruise at about 9–12 km (6–8 miles) high. There are often strong winds at these heights, which can make flights turbulent, or bumpy.

Planes fly high up, where the air is thinner. This means they can travel easier and faster, and burn less fuel.

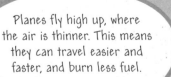

Exosphere

Scientists divide our atmosphere into five main layers. The exosphere is the outermost layer before outer space begins.

Astronauts have flown out several times to service the Hubble Space Telescope.

Hubble Space Telescope
Launched in 1990, this space telescope travels around the Earth, taking amazing photographs of distant stars and galaxies.

Thermosphere

This layer protects us by absorbing a lot of the dangerous energy from the Sun, such as X-rays.

International Space Station
This space station has a crew of up to six astronauts. Each stays about six months, looking after the station and doing experiments. It orbits the Earth once every 90 minutes.

Mesosphere

Most space rocks that enter the atmosphere burn up in the mesosphere. The top of this layer is the coldest part of the Earth's atmosphere.

Venus's atmosphere

Venus's atmosphere contains thick layers of deadly sulphur-containing clouds. Heat from the Sun becomes trapped below these clouds. This makes Venus the hottest planet in the Solar System.

Venus's clouds trap heat below them.

The gas carbon dioxide makes up 96.5% of Venus's atmosphere.

Stratosphere

The stratosphere contains the ozone layer. Ozone is a form of oxygen. It stops harmful ultraviolet rays from the Sun reaching the Earth.

Troposphere

All of our weather happens in the troposphere. It contains most of the air we breathe and a lot of water, including clouds.

The Moon

The Moon is a small, rocky world that is orbiting, or travelling around, the Earth. Let's take a closer look.

Last manned Moon landing

Apollo 15
30 July 1971

Apollo 17
11 December 1972

Do you like my space buggy? The proper name for it is a lunar roving vehicle and it runs on batteries.

Apollo 11
20 July 1969

First Moon landing

Apollo 16
21 April 1972

Apollo 12
19 November 1969

Apollo 14
5 February 1971

Moon crater

Moon landings

Humans first set foot on the Moon in 1969. The flags show where each Moon mission touched down on the surface.

There is no air on the Moon, so astronauts have to wear spacesuits so they can breathe.

Orbiting the Earth

The Moon travels around the Earth about once every 27 days. The Moon appears to change shape in the sky depending on which parts of it are lit by the Sun.

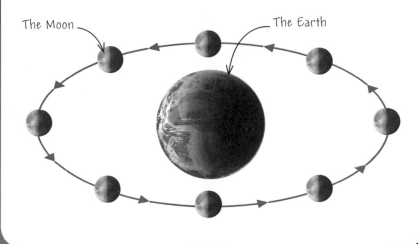

The Moon

The Earth

Apollo spacecraft

The Saturn V rocket is the largest and most powerful rocket ever built.

Rockets travel at about 35,400 kph (22,000 mph). That's pretty fast!

Rocket power

To get to the Moon, humans had to first develop a rocket powerful enough to launch the Apollo spacecrafts into space.

Ladies and gentlemen, I present the *Saturn V* rocket!

The heat produced by a rocket could heat 85,000 homes for a day!

The water cycle

All the water on Earth moves around in a cycle. It rises into the air as moisture and clouds. Rain and snow bring it back to the Earth. It then flows along rivers into the oceans, and the cycle goes on.

The Sun plays a key part in the water cycle. It heats the Earth, causing liquid water to become gas.

Water droplets freeze into ice crystals in very high clouds.

Clouds

As water vapour rises, it cools into tiny liquid droplets, which gather to form clouds. This process is called condensation.

Water has been used to transport people and goods for thousands of years.

Evaporation

Oceans, rivers, and lakes are warmed by the Sun. As they heat up, liquid water at the surface turns into water vapour, which is a gas. This process is called evaporation.

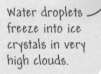

Seawater contains minerals, which is why it tastes very salty.

Rain and snow

When a cloud holds enough water droplets or ice crystals, it makes rain or snow. This water falls back to Earth.

Winter sports such as skiing rely on a good amount of snowfall!

Rainwater is almost pure water, except where it has been polluted by fumes from vehicles and factories.

Back to the sea

Rainwater flows over and under the Earth, slowly making its way back to the oceans. The water picks up minerals on its journey.

Dams are built to break the flow of rivers. We do this to create lakes, generate electricity, or prevent floods.

Groundwater is water in the soil or rocks in the ground. It may flow in underground rivers.

Solids, liquids, and gases

Everything around us is a solid, liquid, or gas. They are all made of something we call "matter". This, in turn, is made up of tiny particles called atoms and molecules.

Liquids

If you can pour something, then it's probably a liquid. Liquids take on the shape of the container they're in. However, they're hard to squash down.

The molecules in a liquid are close but aren't held together as strongly as in a solid. This lets them move past each other, or flow.

Gases

Gases are all around us – the air is made up of gases. A gas will fill any container and can be squashed. Most gases are invisible.

Gas molecules are spread out and move about very quickly.

Condensation

When a gas cools, it turns into a liquid. This is condensation. If you breathe out water vapour onto a cold surface, such as a window, it condenses into water droplets.

Solids

Solids feel firm and are hard to squash. This book is solid, and so are things that you can hold, wear, or sit on.

The particles in a solid are packed together so tightly that they make a fixed shape.

Evaporation

When they are heated, molecules jump out of liquids and become gas. This is called evaporation.

Freezing

A liquid freezes to a solid at a temperature called the freezing point.

Melting

When a solid heats up, its particles vibrate. When it reaches a temperature called the melting point, its particles break free and become liquid.

The weather

The weather affects what people do everyday. One of the reasons it happens is because the Sun heats up the air, causing it to move around. This creates lots of different types of weather.

Thunder and lightning

Thunderstorms are electrical storms that normally happen in hot, humid weather. Lightning is like a giant electrical spark. Thunder is the sound caused by lightning.

Snow

When cloud temperatures are 0°C (32°F) or below, water droplets in the clouds freeze. They form delicate ice crystals and fall as snow!

> Snowploughs clear heavy snowfall to make travel easier.

> Can you paint all the colours of the rainbow?

Rain

Clouds are made up of millions of water droplets that fall as rain when they get too heavy. Rainbows form when it is raining and sunny at the same time!

Snow chains are put on winter tyres to give vehicles more grip.

Sun

Some parts of the Earth get more sunshine than others. That's why it's cold at the North Pole and hot in the Caribbean.

Weather satellites

Weather satellites help forecasters to see what the weather is doing. This makes it easier to predict how it might move or change in the near future.

These satellites watch storms as they move across the Earth.

Fog

Tiny water droplets hanging in the air create cloud at ground level. This is called fog and it is a form of water vapour. Thick fog can make it hard to see into the distance.

Special instruments help pilots to land planes safely in fog.

Wind

Wind is caused by warm air rising and cold air rushing in to take its place.

Dangerous planet

The top, rocky layer of the Earth is made up of gigantic plates that float on a layer of hot rock. Where these plates meet, earthquakes and volcanoes are common.

Tsunamis

Earthquakes happen underwater, too. When they occur, it can cause water levels to rise and create gigantic waves called tsunamis. They travel at great speeds and can cause a lot of destruction.

Seismographs record the movement of the Earth.

Earthquake strength is measured using the Richter scale. Over eight on the scale is a very strong earthquake!

The point on the ground directly above the red dot is the epicentre. This is where the most damage occurs.

In places where earthquakes are common, buildings are designed to wobble but not collapse.

Earthquakes

When plates collide or scrape against each other, pressure builds up. After this pressure is released, shock waves travel through the ground. This is known as an earthquake and it can be very dangerous.

The red dot is called the hypocentre. This is where an earthquake begins.

Volcanoes

Volcanoes are openings in the ground where hot, melted rock, called magma, escapes from deep underground. It's best not to be near a volcano when it's erupting!

When magma flows out of a volcano it is called lava.

Scientists take measurements of changes in the volcano's shape, vibrations, and gases to try to predict when the next eruption might be.

A thermometer measures lava temperature, which gets as hot as 700–1,300°C (1,300–2,400°F)!

Lava can ooze from cracks in the sides of a volcano.

The main vent is the biggest opening for magma to escape.

A magma chamber is a pool of hot, melted rock.

Fish

Fish live in water, breathe in oxygen using gills, and are cold-blooded. They have fins to help them swim.

Reptiles

Reptiles have scaly skin and are cold-blooded. Most lay eggs. Apart from snakes, almost all other types of reptile have four legs.

Cold-blooded animals sunbathe to warm up their bodies.

Pandas spend 16 hours each day eating bamboo.

Birds

Birds have feathers, wings, and a hollow skeleton. Most can fly, but some, such as penguins, cannot. Birds lay eggs and are warm-blooded.

Amphibians

Amphibians, such as frogs and newts, live in water and on land. They are cold-blooded and have moist skin.

Mammals

Mammals have hair and are warm-blooded. They give birth to live babies, which they feed with milk. You are a mammal!

Vertebrates

These animals have a backbone and a skull. A strong skeleton inside their bodies lets them grow larger than invertebrates.

Animals

There are millions of different types of animal in the world. Scientists divide them into two groups – vertebrates and invertebrates. However, all animals have things in common, such as breathing air, moving around to find food, and sensing the world.

Less than 5% of all the different types of animal are vertebrates. There are many, many more types of invertebrate.

Crustaceans
Most crustaceans, such as crabs, lobsters, and shrimps, live in or around water. They have hard shells.

If a starfish loses one of its arms, it can grow a new one to replace it!

Echinoderms
These spiny-skinned animals do not have brains! They include starfish and sea urchins, and live on the ocean floor.

Arachnids
Spiders, ticks, mites, scorpions, and daddy longlegs are all types of arachnid. They all have eight legs.

Molluscs
Molluscs have soft bodies. Many, including snails and clams, have hard shells. Most live in water – for example octopuses – but those living on land must keep damp.

Insects
Insects have six legs, two antennae, or feelers, on their head, an exoskeleton, and many can fly. There are more than one million known types of insect.

Invertebrates
These animals don't have a backbone, or spine. Some, such as slugs, are soft and squishy. Others, such as insects, have an exoskeleton, which is a kind of shell.

Octopuses are the cleverest invertebrates. It's been found that they can solve problems to get food.

Small and tall
Animals come in all shapes and sizes. Some are so small you need a microscope to see them. Bumblebee bats are the smallest mammals, while giraffes are the tallest animals in the world!

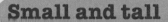

Paper clip	Bumblebee bat	Adult man	Giraffe
3.2 cm (1.2 in)	4 cm (1.57 in)	1.7 m (5.8 ft)	6 m (20 ft)

Plants

From daisies to palm trees, there are thousands of different types of plant in the world. They provide us with oxygen to breathe, many kinds of food, and wood to make homes and furniture.

Plants get their energy from sunlight.

Farming

Farmers grow crops, such as corn, wheat, fruit, vegetables, and cotton. They give their crops fertilizers, which are extra nutrients, to make them grow bigger and faster.

Engineers and scientists change crops to improve them – for example, so they don't get diseases.

Leaves
A plant's leaves absorb sunlight, which is used to make food for the plant. The leaves also release oxygen into the air.

Stamens
These parts of the flower make a fine powder called pollen.

Stigma
This part of the flower has a skicky end. It collects pollen to make seeds.

Some plants have flowers, some lose their leaves in the winter, and some even eat insects!

Plant parts
Many plants are made up of similar parts. They have roots in the soil, strong stems, leaves growing from the stems, and sometimes flowers.

Stem
The stem supports the plant, and both water and food travel along it. We get wood from tree stems.

Roots
The roots anchor the plant and absorb water and nutrients from the soil.

Butterflies can carry pollen long distances.

Fruit

Fruit have seeds inside them. When animals eat fruit, the seeds come out in their poo. This way, the seeds are carried to new areas, where they grow into new plants.

Insects

Insects spread pollen between flowers so that they can make seeds. Many flowers attract insects with a sweet liquid called nectar. When they come to drink it, the pollen sticks to them.

Bees are the most important pollen carriers.

Fungi

Mushrooms and toadstools are not plants. They belong to a kingdom of living things called fungi. They feed on living or dead plants and animals and soak up their nutrients.

Mushroom

Evolution

Over time, animals and plants change, or adapt, so they can survive in their environment for longer and have more babies. This is called evolution. Evolution isn't a quick process – it takes millions of years!

55 million years ago

Whale evolution

Incredibly, the ancestors of whales lived on land! Over time, they grew bigger and bigger and moved to different places, including the ocean.

Pakicetus
Pakicetus lived on land, possibly near water. It had four hoofed feet and sharp teeth for chewing flesh or plants.

The powerful long tail helped to steer in water.

Natural selection means that some living things are better at surviving than others.

50 million years ago

Ambulocetus
Ambulocetus evolved from pakicetus. It lived in water and hunted like a crocodile.

Short legs and padded feet were perfect for paddling in water.

Darwin
Charles Darwin was a scientist who studied how animals and plants changed over time. He came up with the theory of evolution to explain what he saw.

Wide tail

Bowhead whale

By the time the bowhead whale evolved, it had grown enormously in size, with an appetite to match. They feed on a massive 100,000 kg (220,000 lb) of plankton a year!

Today

Bowhead whales can survive for more than 100 years!

Giant flippers

Palaeontologists are scientists who study fossils – the remains of ancient animals and plants.

Long, pointed snout

Breeding

It's hard to imagine that a chihuahua evolved from a wolf, but it did! Humans breed dogs for herding, security, companionship, and even for their appearance.

Wolf

Chihuahua

Much smaller legs than ambulocetus

38 million years ago

Dorudon

Twelve million years later, the front feet had evolved into flippers and had become webbed.

The Arctic food web

Animals need food to give them the energy they need to move and think. A food web shows what different animals in a particular place, or habitat, eat – and how they all link together.

Arctic tern

These seabirds catch fish by diving into the water at great speeds. Adults are safe from predators, but their eggs and chicks are not.

Polar bears have white fur so that they blend into their surroundings.

Polar bear

Polar bears are apex predators, which means they eat other animals, such as ringed seals, but no animals eat them.

The killer whale is also known as an orca.

Killer whale

Killer whales hunt in the ocean and also grab unsuspecting seals near the water's edge. They are apex predators, too.

Plant plankton rely on the Sun for energy.

Some plankton are so small they can't be seen with the naked eye.

Arctic cod

These fish are a food source for many marine animals. Arctic cod eat plankton, shrimp, marine worms, and sometimes even each other!

Plankton

Tiny drifting animals and plants called plankton are eaten by Arctic cod and coldwater shrimp.

Ringed seal

This meat-eating animal eats fish, shrimp, and plankton, but is hunted and eaten by polar bears and killer whales.

Draw your own

To draw your own food web, start by choosing a habitat, such as a forest or a desert. Now think about what the animals in that habitat eat and show how they link together.

Coldwater shrimp

Coldwater shrimp live near the ocean floor and mostly eat plankton. They make a tasty snack for seals.

Ecosystems

Plants and animals live and interact with each other and their surroundings in communities called ecosystems. Ecosystems can be as small as a tree trunk or as large as a rainforest.

The biggest coral reef is the Great Barrier Reef off the coast of eastern Australia.

American desert

The deserts of southwest USA are extremely hot but lots of animals and plants live there. Animals avoid the heat of the day by hunting at night, and plants can survive a long time without any rain.

The great horned owl makes its nests on saguaro cactuses, where its eggs will be safe from predators.

Coyotes survive in many different places because they will eat whatever is available!

The sharp spines will put off any egg thieves!

The organ pipe cactus opens its flowers at night.

This rattlesnake will shake the rattle on the end of its tail if it feels threatened.

The saguaro cactus is the largest cactus in the USA.

Under the sea

Coral reefs are amazing underwater structures formed by living creatures. They grow in warm, shallow waters in tropical regions and are home to a dazzling variety of life.

The banded sea krait is a type of sea snake.

Reefs are home to all sorts of fish.

This type of coral is called table coral.

A stinging anemone provides a safe haven for clownfish...

...while clownfish scare off fish who want to eat the anemone!

Mountains

The Himalayan mountain range in Asia is a tough place to live. Animals and plants have to cope with extreme cold, storms, and living at great heights.

Golden eagles have incredible eyesight for spotting prey from great distances.

Snow leopards are incredibly rare. They eat wild sheep and goats.

Pikas are hunted by golden eagles.

Wild goats, like this markhor, munch plants and spread seeds in their dung.

Mount Everest in the Himalayas is the world's highest mountain.

Inside a
rainforest

Tropical rainforests are made up of four different layers. Each one provides a home for different types of animals and plants.

Emergent layer

The tallest trees can reach heights of up to 55 m (180 ft). That's a long way up!

Canopy

The canopy is a thick layer of treetops that is home to animals, birds, and lots of climbing plants.

Sloths move very slowly.

Tree frogs rarely leave the canopy.

Understorey

Short trees and shrubs provide cover for small animals as well as predators such as jaguars.

Pitcher plant

Forest floor

This is the darkest part of the rainforest. It's muddy and covered in leaves that have fallen from the trees above.

Okapi

Scarlet macaw

Sunlight in layers

Each layer of the rainforest gets different amounts of sunlight.

Emergent layer
Full sunlight

Canopy
Lots of sunlight

Understorey
Sunlight and shade

Forest floor
Mostly shade

Blue morpho butterflies are found in the emergent layer.

Gibbons are a type of ape from Asia.

The toucan's beak is so colourful. Why not try to paint a picture of it?

Toucans use their beaks to grab fruit and nuts.

Snakes slither between the layers.

Chameleons can make their skin change colour!

Jaguar

This gigantic flower stinks of rotting flesh to attract flies that will spread its pollen.

Leafcutter ants

Anteater

39

Climate change

Climate is the general weather conditions over a large area. It changes naturally over long periods of time. However, recently Earth's climate has been getting warmer faster than usual.

Polluted planet

Fossil fuels, such as oil and coal, are the buried remains of ancient plants and other living things. Burning them releases harmful gases, especially carbon dioxide (CO_2), into the air. These gases heat up and pollute our planet.

Carbon dioxide is called a "greenhouse gas" as it traps the Sun's energy in our atmosphere, heating the planet.

Factories
Over the last few hundred years, many coal-burning factories were built. They pumped more CO_2 into the atmosphere.

Motor vehicles
Cars and lorries use diesel and petrol as fuel. These fuels are made from oil. Burning them releases CO_2 into the air.

Chopping down forests
Trees soak up CO_2 like a big sponge. By chopping down forests for timber or to make farmland, we take away one of the best ways to remove CO_2 from the air.

A greener future

Scientists and engineers now look for ways to make energy that do not burn fossil fuels. They are especially interested in energy sources that won't ever run out, such as wind and sunlight.

Experts predict that by 2040, one-third of all cars bought will be electric cars.

Solar panels
Solar panels absorb sunlight to make electricity and heat.

Electric cars
These cars run on rechargeable batteries, rather than petrol. Because of this, they don't pollute the air with CO_2 and other harmful gases.

Trees
Planting trees helps to fight climate change because plants absorb CO_2 from the air. They use the carbon to make their own food and grow.

Every tree makes a difference. This little one could live for 200 years!

Effects of climate change

A warmer climate can lead to extreme weather. Big storms are becoming more common, often causing flooding. Climate change is also melting the sea ice covering the Arctic Ocean.

Flooding

Melting Arctic sea ice

Wind farms
Wind turbines make electricity from wind power rather than by burning fossil fuels. Groups of turbines are called wind farms.

Microlife

There are billions of very tiny living things around us, on us, and even inside us! Our eyes can just about see some of this microlife. However, we need to use a microscope to see how amazing they really are.

Dust mites

These blobby creatures eat bits of dead skin found in house dust and mould. They're very hard to see because they're tiny and almost see-through.

Hair lice

These tiny insects live in hair, usually children's. They bite the scalp to feed on blood. However, apart from causing itching, they are not harmful.

Hair lice have two antennae, or feelers, on their heads.

Dust mites have many little hairs, called setae.

Hair lice glue their eggs, called nits, to shafts of hair.

Tardigrades

Also called water bears, these little animals live in wet places, such as mud. They are super tough, can survive in space, and can go without food and water for more than 30 years!

Tardigrades have four pairs of chunky legs with tiny claws. Their name means "slow stepper".

Plankton

Plankton are living things that drift about in oceans, rivers, and lakes. Some are microscopic, or really tiny, but others, such as jellyfish, are much bigger. Many sea and freshwater animals eat plankton.

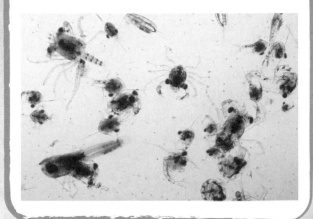

Bacteria

Bacteria are microscopic living things, made of just one cell each. They are much smaller than the cells that make up our bodies. In fact, our bodies contain billions of bacteria! Some of these bacteria are useful, supplying us with important nutrients. However, others can cause nasty diseases.

This bacterium has started to split into two new cells.

Viruses

Viruses are tiny things that can make people, animals, and plants ill. They enter cells and then make copies of themselves. Flu, colds, and measles are all caused by viruses.

The human body

An adult human body contains 206 bones, 650 muscles, and trillions of tiny building blocks called cells. Each part of the body has a different job to do, but they all work together to keep the body running smoothly.

The human body is made up of systems. The nervous system controls how we think, feel, and move, the immune system fights sickness, and the digestive system turns food into energy.

Our supercomputer, the brain, controls our thoughts and actions.

Brain

Organs

Our body is made up of lots of different organs. The organs that help us digest food include the stomach, the liver, the intestines, and the kidneys. Even our skin is an organ!

The heart pumps blood around our body.

The liver has more than 500 jobs. We wouldn't be able to survive for more than two days without it!

Heart

Lungs

Liver

Kidneys

Stomach

Large intestine

Small intestine

Lungs transport oxygen from the air into our bloodstream.

X-rays are not just used to look at bones, they also scan luggage at airports.

Muscles

Muscles are the stretchy cords connected to our bones that allow us to move. Some muscles work without us having to think about them, while others are controlled by our brain.

Skin

Skin is the waterproof outer layer that stops us from injuring or infecting our insides. It is the biggest organ in the human body, making up 15% of our weight!

Bones

Newborn babies have more than 300 bones. By the time we reach adulthood, some bones have joined together to make 206 in total. They fit together to form the skeleton, protecting our inner organs and keeping us upright.

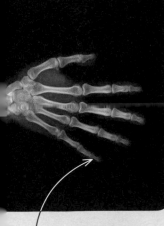

X-rays allow us to see what our bones look like.

Blood

The heart pumps blood around our body through tubes called blood vessels. Blood transports oxygen to parts of the body and fights germs.

Veins and arteries are blood vessels that carry blood to and from the heart.

Two sides

The brain has two sides. The left side controls the right side of our body, while the right side is in charge of the left side of the body!

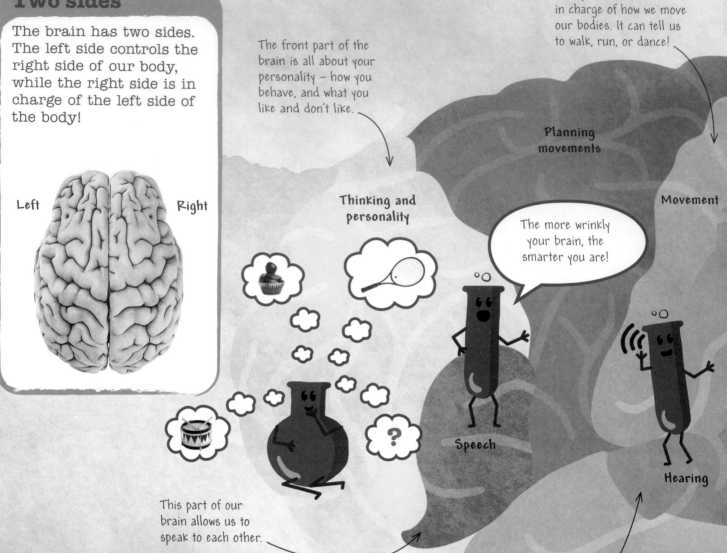

Left   Right

The front part of the brain is all about your personality – how you behave, and what you like and don't like.

This part of the brain is in charge of how we move our bodies. It can tell us to walk, run, or dance!

Planning movements

Movement

Thinking and personality

The more wrinkly your brain, the smarter you are!

Speech

Hearing

This part of our brain allows us to speak to each other.

Memory

You figure out what different sounds are in this part of the brain.

This part of your brain is where you keep all of your memories, like the first time you rode a bike or your last birthday party.

Think
about it

Your brain may look like a big wobbly ball of jelly, but it works like an amazing supercomputer. It sits in your head and allows you to see, hear, talk, move, feel, think, imagine, and remember.

Every time you touch something a message goes to this part of the brain.

Being able to understand our surroundings helps us to make good decisions about how to move around.

Touch

Awareness of space

Understanding emotions, like happiness or sadness, helps us to respond well to other people.

Emotional understanding

Making images

Artificial intelligence

Computers can be taught to think and make decisions like humans. This is called artificial intelligence (AI). Mobile phones use AI to help answer any questions you might have or tell you what's in your diary.

What's the weather like today?

It's raining. Take an umbrella!

Seeing

Our brain receives information from our eyes and makes sense of what we're seeing.

Coordination
This bit of the brain helps us to move smoothly. It's useful for things such as walking and writing.

Nervous system

We have a huge network of nerves inside us, which link the brain and the spinal cord to the other parts of the body.

The spinal cord carries messages to and from the brain.

The senses

Our senses let us understand the world around us. They tell us what's safe and what's dangerous, and let us see and hear each other. Special receptors in our bodies help us to sense our world.

Sight
A lens inside each of our eyes focuses light onto the back of the eye. There, receptors sense brightness and colours.

The main senses
Sight, smell, touch, taste, and hearing are our five main senses. However, we also have other senses that help us survive.

Smell
Tiny receptors inside the nose pick up many different odours. Smell is closely linked to the sense of taste.

Touch
The skin contains many receptors that react when we touch things.

Taste
Taste buds on the top of the tongue sense five different flavours. These are salty, sweet, sour, bitter, and a savoury flavour called umami.

A human eye contains more than 125 million receptors.

Pain
We have receptors in our bodies that let us feel pain.

Heat
Receptors in the skin let us feel heat.

Needing the toilet
Receptors deeper inside our bodies let us know when it's time to go to the toilet.

Other senses
There are many other kinds of receptor in our bodies, checking what's happening outside and inside us.

Hearing
Sounds travel into the ears and are sensed by receptors in the inner ears, inside our head. The inner ears also give us our sense of balance.

Echolocation

Bats have a special sense called echolocation, which they use to catch flying insects at night. They make calls and listen for echoes as the calls bounce off the insects. This tells the bats exactly where the insects are. In a similar way, submarines use technology called SONAR to find other objects under the sea.

Bat

Submarine

Technology

Technology uses science to create inventions. Often the aim of these inventions is to make our lives easier. Engineers use a series of steps to come up with new and exciting products.

Tubes make great linking devices.

This tube looks like it will be large enough to pick up tiny bits of dirt and big pieces of paper.

1 A problem

The first thing to do is to find the problem that needs solving. Ask questions to find out as much as you can so that you can properly understand the whole problem.

Hmm, this cat makes so much mess! I wish I had a way of easily cleaning up...

2

3

Research

Once you've decided on your best idea, it's time to research. Find out what materials you will need to build your design.

Wheels will make it easier to move a heavy object.

4

Building

The first thing that you build is called a prototype. You'll be able to see your idea coming to life and be able to spot anything you can tweak to make it better.

Engineers use lots of different tools.

Building your invention in stages makes it easier.

5

Improving the design

After you've made your invention, test it over and over again. You might come up with new ideas for how to make an improved version!

Someone could trip over a cord or wire.

Next time we could try to design a vacuum cleaner without a cord.

Ideas

Think of as many different ideas as you can at the start. Write or draw them all down so you can see everything in front of you. It's great to work in a team to come up with as many ideas as possible.

Simple machines

Machines help us to transport, fix, and power things. We have designed lots of different types of machine to carry out jobs, and many are surprisingly simple.

By pulling down, I lift the weight up! Clever, eh?

Wheel

These round parts help machines to get about. Different wheels are used for different surfaces. Grooved wheels suit slippery ground.

The grooves grip the ground.

Screw

Pointy metal screws hold things together. They are placed inside both parts that you want to join. You use a screwdriver to twist and push them in.

The screw turns into place.

Pulley

If an object is very heavy, you can use a pulley to lift it. A rope is passed over the top of a wheel and attached to the weight. You pull on the rope to lift the weight.

The weight is hooked onto the pulley.

Gears

Gears are connected wheels with sticky-out bits called spokes. A smaller, lighter wheel is turned by hand. The spokes catch the heavier wheel to push it round.

This wheel is too heavy to move by hand.

You wouldn't be able to lift these weights by hand.

Lever

You use a lever to lift things. An example of a lever is a plank balanced on a single point called a fulcrum.

If I push down here, the weights lift up!

The fulcrum is near the middle.

Wedge

A triangular wedge is used to split things in two. The wedge is swung downwards into the object.

An axe is a type of wedge.

A wheeled cart carries the object.

Ramp

To raise or lower an object that is too heavy to lift, we can push it along smooth ramps that slope upwards or downwards.

Time zones

The world is divided into 24 different time zones, one hour apart. When you're having your breakfast, someone else in the world is having their dinner. Russia is so big it has 11 time zones!

Travelling by plane across different time zones can confuse our bodies and cause tiredness, headaches, and problems sleeping. This is called jet lag.

The Greenwich Meridian Line is the centre of all time zones. It is where east meets west.

Greenwich Meridian Line

What's the time? Well, that depends on where you are on Earth. It can be midnight in one place and midday in another!

Body clock

We, and other animals, have a built-in, natural body clock. This tells us when we should be awake and when we should sleep. Our body clock is linked to light and darkness.

Time

We use time to work out when things happen – from dates in history to what time you have to get up in the morning. We measure time in seconds, minutes, hours, days, and years.

If I walk from one time zone to another, am I time travelling?

Months and years

One year on Earth is 365 days long. This is the time it takes the Earth to travel around the Sun. One month is roughly how long it takes for the Moon to travel around the Earth.

Calendars help us to keep track of days and months.

September
1 2 3 4 5 6
7 8 9 10 11 12 13
14 15 16 17 18 19 20
21 22 23 24 25 26
27 28 29 30

The International Date Line is an imaginary line in the middle of the Pacific Ocean. It separates one day from the next.

The International Date Line

Day   Night

How shall I tell the time? Sundials use shadows, analogue clocks have faces and hands that tick, and digital clocks display the time on a screen.

Analogue clock

Digital clock

Sundial

Telling time

People have been telling the time for thousands of years. But it wasn't until quite recently – 1884 to be exact – that time zones were established.

Measuring

To find out how hot, how big, or how heavy something is we have to measure it. Special tools help us to get accurate measurements. This is especially important when building a house or baking a cake!

Height

How tall are you? Get someone to measure you with a tape measure. Now measure a friend. Who is the tallest?

Temperature

We measure temperature with thermometers. They tell you exactly how hot something is.

Water boils at 100°C (212°F).

Tape measures, rulers, and even digital lasers measure height and distance.

Chefs must use precise measurements of temperature and time when cooking.

Time

In the past, people told the time using the Sun and the Moon. Today, we use clocks as our main timekeeping device.

We divide time into seconds, minutes, and hours.

Graphs make it easy to see how things are changing.

Keep a record

Scientists note down measurements regularly, so they can see how things change over time. They use graphs and charts to compare measurements.

Litres and millilitres are used to measure liquid.

In the USA, people often use cups to measure volume.

Volume

Volume is the amount of space something takes up. Volume measures size, not weight. Two objects might have the same volume but very different weights.

Kitchen scales help us weigh ingredients for cooking.

Weight

Weight tells us how heavy something is. If you have some scales at home you can weigh yourself!

Using numbers

We use numbers to count, measure, and compare amounts. Scientists and engineers have to be good at maths – or their experiments and inventions won't work!

Counting

Counting different things allows us to compare them. For example, you could compare the number of spots on different ladybirds to see which type is the most common.

Ladybirds' spots can vary in number.

A

B

C

A 𝍸𝍸𝍸 ||

B 𝍸𝍸𝍸 𝍸𝍸𝍸 𝍸𝍸𝍸 |

C ||

Tally charts have been used since the Stone Age!

This could take a while...

1ˢᵗ

2ⁿᵈ

3ʳᵈ

Addition

Addition is usually the first type of maths we learn. When adding numbers, it doesn't matter what order they are in, the answer will be the same.

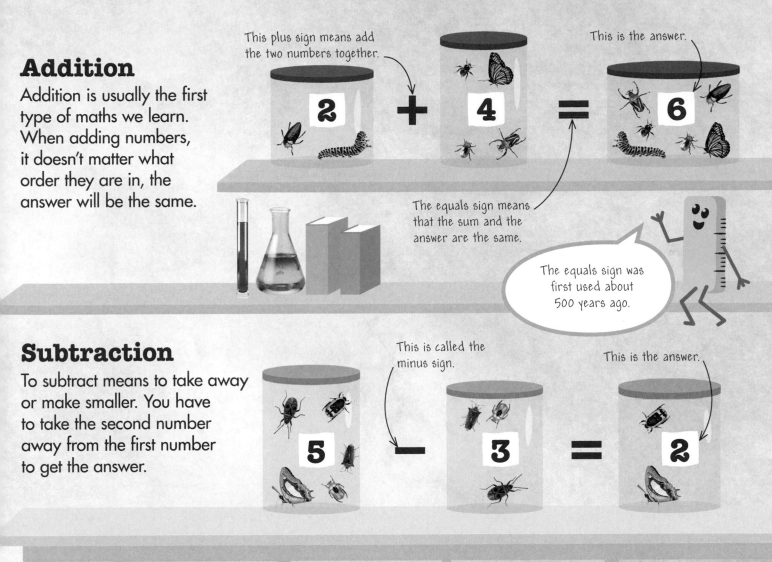

This plus sign means add the two numbers together.

This is the answer.

2 + 4 = 6

The equals sign means that the sum and the answer are the same.

The equals sign was first used about 500 years ago.

Subtraction

To subtract means to take away or make smaller. You have to take the second number away from the first number to get the answer.

This is called the minus sign.

This is the answer.

5 - 3 = 2

2nd place is the silver medal position.

2nd

The winner of the race comes in 1st place.

3rd

1st

Sports events reward 3rd place, too.

Positions

Ordinal numbers tell you about the position, order, or sequence of something. 1st, 2nd, and 3rd are examples of ordinal numbers.

Materials

Everything around us is made of materials. Different materials have different qualities. Some, such as metals, are hard and strong. Others, such as plastics, can be easily moulded, or shaped. Engineers, scientists, and designers create and use materials in lots of different ways.

Plastic

Plastic is a human-made material that has many different qualities. It is light, waterproof, and can be hard or soft.

Ceramics

Ceramics are hard but break easily. They can cope with really high temperatures – space shuttles have ceramic tiles to protect them from extreme heat.

People have been making ceramic pots and vases for thousands of years.

Glass

Glass is made from sand. It's useful in windows because it can keep the weather out but still allow us to see through it.

Metal

At very high temperatures, metals become soft and can be reshaped.

Metals are usually strong and easy to shape when heated. They are conductors, which means electricity and heat can travel through them. Some metals are magnetic.

Plastic is easy to mould into lots of different shapes.

Fabric

Fabrics can be dyed or patterned to make beautiful clothes.

Fabrics can be made from natural things, such as sheep's wool, or be created in a factory. Scientists have created protective fabrics that are waterproof or that block the Sun's rays.

Uh-oh! I'll be in pain if I break this pane!

Carbon fibre is a very strong composite used to make surfboards.

Composites

Combinations of two or more materials are called composites. They have the best qualities of the materials used to make them.

Wood

Wood is a natural material that comes from trees. It is used to make homes and furniture. Different types of wood have different colours and grains, or patterns.

Wood is used to make paper and toilet roll, too!

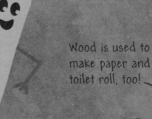

Building bridges

Bridges are designed by engineers to get us from one place to another as quickly as possible. They can cross canyons, rivers, roads, and train tracks.

Cantilever

A cantilever is a structure that is only supported at one end. To create a cantilever bridge, lots of these structures are joined together.

The cables can make interesting patterns.

Cable-stayed

A cable-stayed bridge has one or two towers. Cables fan directly down from these towers to the bridge base, holding it up.

Suspension bridges can span great distances.

Suspension

In a suspension bridge, steel wires connect two tall towers that are sunk deep into the ground. The crossing hangs from these towers.

Log bridge

A log bridge is the most ancient form of bridge. It is made from trees that have fallen or are cut down on purpose.

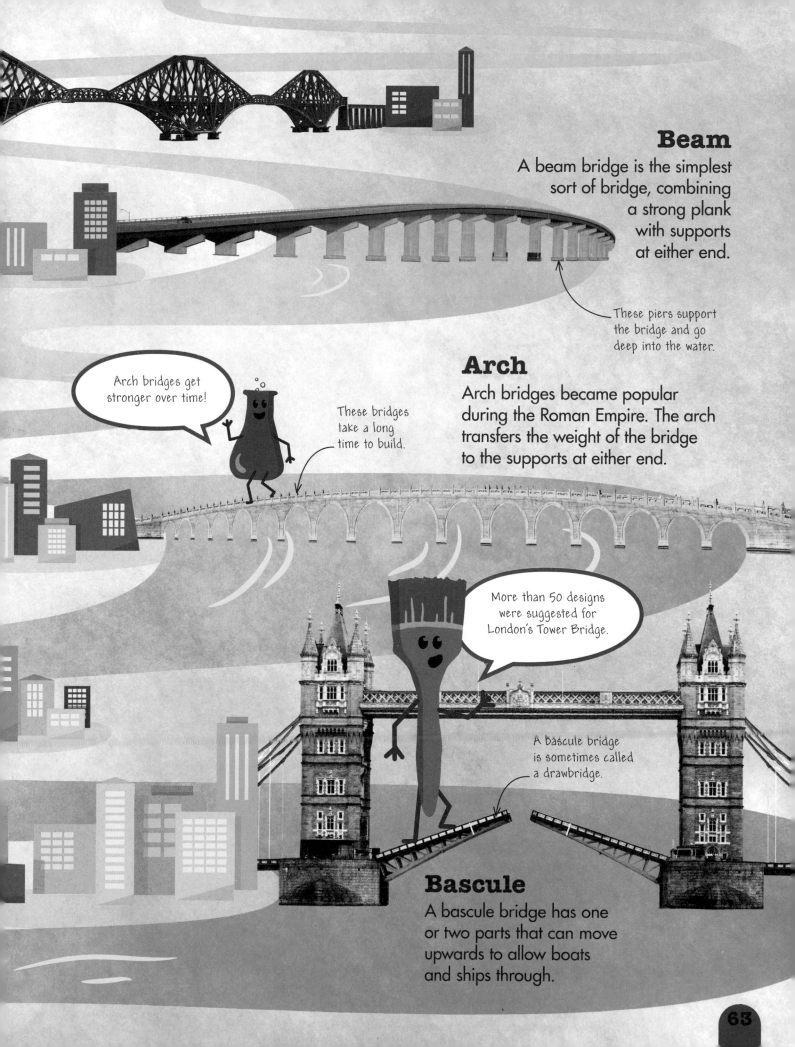

Beam

A beam bridge is the simplest sort of bridge, combining a strong plank with supports at either end.

These piers support the bridge and go deep into the water.

Arch

Arch bridges became popular during the Roman Empire. The arch transfers the weight of the bridge to the supports at either end.

These bridges take a long time to build.

Bascule

A bascule bridge has one or two parts that can move upwards to allow boats and ships through.

A bascule bridge is sometimes called a drawbridge.

Take to the skies

In order to fly, you have to overcome the force of gravity pulling you towards the ground. Helicopters and aeroplanes use rotors, wings, and engines to soar through the air.

In a hovering helicopter, all the forces balance exactly.

Tail rotor

Drag
Drag, or air resistance, is the force that pulls the helicopter backwards. Drag increases as the helicopter moves faster.

Without a tail rotor the helicopter would turn in circles!

Forces of flight

There are four main forces working on a helicopter as it flies. Drag tries to slow it down, gravity tries to bring it back to Earth, lift raises it upwards, and thrust propels it forwards.

Helicopters can fly backwards!

Dreams of flying

The Italian artist and inventor Leonardo da Vinci was fascinated with flying. He studied birds and drew many imaginary flying devices, such as a wing-flapping machine for humans.

Da Vinci's wing design

Lift
Lift holds the helicopter in the air and is created by its rotors. It is the force that is the opposite of gravity.

Planes use their wings to create lift.

Sycamore seeds are also called "helicopter seeds" because of the way they spin.

Main rotor

Search and rescue helicopters have night-vision cameras.

Thrust
Thrust is the force that pushes the helicopter forwards. It is created by the helicopter's engine.

Gravity
Gravity pulls the helicopter in a downward direction, towards the centre of the Earth.

Cockpit
The cockpit contains all of the instruments and controls that allow the pilot to fly the helicopter.

The weight of the metal ship, plus the air inside it, is less than the upward force of the water.

Why does the anchor sink while the ship floats?

The heavy, dense, metal anchor is specially designed to sink in water.

Floating

A huge metal ship can float because it's full of air. The amount of space the ship takes up weighs less than the equivalent, or same, amount of water.

Water pushes against the weight of the ship. The upward force of the water is greater than the ship's weight, so the ship floats.

The upward force of the water is less than the weight of the anchor.

Sinking

Objects sink if their weight is greater than the force of the water pushing them upwards. Dense materials, such as metal and stone, usually sink, unless they have air inside them.

Scuba divers use inflatable jackets and weights to move up or down, or stay at the same depth underwater.

Floating and sinking

Why is a massive ship able to float when a small pebble quickly sinks? It depends on which is greater – the weight of the object in the water or the upward force of the water pushing against it.

Submarines can stay underwater, with people living on them, for many months!

Tanks fill with air to make the submarine rise.

At the surface
The submarine's tanks are filled with air when it's floating at the surface.

The largest submarines are 175 m (575 ft) long and have 160 crew members.

Tanks fill with water to make the submarine sink.

Changing weight

Submarines can change their weight. They have tanks that can be filled with water to make the submarine heavier, or filled with air to make it lighter. This way, they can sink or rise.

Going down
When the submarine takes water into its tanks, the extra weight makes the submarine heavier compared to the water around it. The submarine then sinks.

Friction

When two surfaces rub against each other it creates a force called friction. Let's take a look at a bicycle to see friction in action.

There's friction between your clothes and the seat. This stops you from falling off!

Friction between the brake pads and the wheels slows the bike down.

Rubbing your hands together creates friction, which produces heat.

Rubber or metal pedals create friction to stop your feet from sliding.

The wheel moves across the ground.

Bike chains are greased with oil.

Friction with the ground slows the wheel.

Oil reduces friction so the chain moves smoothly.

How friction works

No surfaces are completely smooth – up-close they are covered in tiny bumps. When these catch on each other they slow down the moving object, in this case a tyre, helping it to grip the road.

As a parachute falls, the air pushes back up against it. This is a type of friction called air resistance.

Skis are flat, smooth, and lightweight. This allows them to slide over icy surfaces easily, because less friction occurs when surfaces are smooth.

Handlebars are often textured to create friction. This makes them easy to grip.

The lighter the bike, the quicker it moves!

Mountain bikes have thick, grooved tyres to grip uneven trails. Racing bikes have thin, smoother tyres to move fast on roads.

Tyres are now often made from Kevlar® to stop punctures. Kevlar® is a very strong and light human-made material.

69

Electricity

Electricity is a type of energy that is used to power many everyday objects, from light bulbs to TVs. Take a look around your home and see how many electrical devices you can spot.

Electrical gadgets make my life easier at home! Although I wish someone else would do the hoovering...

Power lines carry electricity over long distances – from power stations into our homes.

Without electricity, vacuum cleaners wouldn't be able to suck up dirt.

Batteries

Batteries are small objects that can create their own electricity. They're often used for remote controls, radios, and torches.

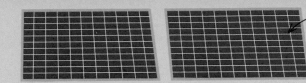

Switch

Switches control most electrical things around the home. Turn them on to start the flow of electricity, or turn them off to stop it.

Lights should be turned off when not needed!

The battery in my toothbrush can be recharged and used many times, so my teeth are always sparkling clean!

Wires

Metal is a conductor. This means that it lets electricity pass through it. Wires have metal inside them and plastic on the outside. The plastic is an insulator that stops electricity from escaping.

Metal

Plastic

Light bulb

Can you imagine life before the light bulb? It wasn't so long ago that people used candles and oil lamps to work once it got dark. Now we have light with the flick of a switch!

Tablets, computers, and mobile phones give off light, too.

71

The Internet

The Internet is a worldwide network of computers that are connected together. Using the Internet you can chat with friends in faraway places, order a new pair of shoes, watch the latest blockbuster, and much more!

A smartwatch links to your smartphone using the Internet and lets you make calls, pay for things, and play music.

Smartphones are computers that we carry in our pockets.

We can use the Internet to make video calls – even to people in space!

Most smartphones can tell you how long it will take you to get somewhere!

Social networking

Social networking is a way of using your computer to talk to other people all over the world. It's important to stay safe online, so only connect with people you know and never give out personal details, such as your address or phone number.

Webcams can be used to video chat with people, or can be set up to study areas, like nature reserves, for a long time.

Maps

Smartphones have clever systems that can tell exactly where you are on Earth. From this, they can tell you the best way to get from one place to another using maps.

Vans drive all over the world with Internet deliveries.

Speedy parcels

You can buy presents and get them delivered straight to your friends and family.

You can even get same-day delivery!

Shopping

Lots of people use the Internet to buy food, clothes, books, and more without having to leave the house. It can all be ordered, paid for, and delivered straight to your front door!

Since its invention, the Internet has completely changed the way we live!

Research

The Internet lets us find out more information on our favourite subjects and learn more about the things that interest us.

Pick a topic and see how much you can find out about it online.

Viruses

When a computer virus spreads it can slow a computer down or stop it working altogether. One of the main ways a virus spreads is when we download things from the Internet.

Streaming

We can use the Internet to watch TV shows, films, and funny cat videos, or listen to music by our favourite singers or bands.

Robots

Robots are machines that can do jobs for us. They can be programmed by a computer to work alone, or they can be controlled by humans. Robotics is one of the most exciting areas of technology, with new robots being invented all the time.

Humanoid robots

Some robots are designed to copy the way humans look, move, and feel. These humanoid robots can do basic tasks and keep people company.

pepper

Image courtesy of Softbank Robotics

Entertainment

Robots can entertain us. Some robots sing, dance, or play musical instruments. Pet robots are very popular, and some theme parks have huge robot dinosaurs.

Robotic dogs act like real dogs. They wag their tail and bark.

Body parts

Robotic body parts are attached to people with missing arms or legs. This lets them carry out everyday activities that they might not have been able to do before.

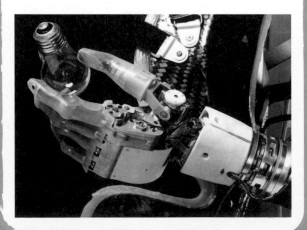

Mobile robots

Robots are perfect for working in extreme conditions. They can go down cracks in glaciers, travel to the bottom of the sea, and even work in space!

A drone is a flying robot that can take photographs and videos.

Security robots

Security robots are fitted with cameras and sensors. They can patrol large areas, such as shopping centres, on their own at any time of day or night.

If this roving security robot detects an intruder, it will alert its owner.

A robotic vacuum cleaner moves around by itself.

Domestic robots

Robots can carry out the boring chores we don't always enjoy doing. They can wash floors, clean windows, iron shirts, and even clean a cat's litter box!

Glossary

absorb
To soak up or take in

asteroid
Small, rocky object that travels around, or orbits, the Sun

astronaut
Someone who is trained to travel and work in a spacecraft

atoms
Tiny particles that make up everything around us

axis
Imaginary line that passes through the centre of a planet or star, around which the planet or star turns

black hole
Object in space with such a strong force of gravity that nothing can escape it, not even light

calendar
Chart showing the days, weeks, and months of a year

comet
Object made of dust and ice that orbits the Sun, developing a tail as it gets near to the Sun

dwarf planet
Small type of planet, such as Pluto

electrical storm
Storm with thunder and lightning

galaxy
Huge group of stars, gas, and dust

gills
Organs of fish and some amphibians that lets them breathe underwater

glacier
Large mass of ice that moves slowly down a slope

laser
Narrow beam of strong light

magnetic
Word used to describe the force created by magnets, which can pull certain metals towards them

magnetic field
Force field surrounding a planet, star, or galaxy

marine
Word used to describe animals or plants that live in or near the sea

molecule

Group of atoms stuck together

moon

Object made of rock, or rock and ice, that travels around a planet

mould

Type of fungus that grows in damp places

online

Connected to the Internet

organ

Part of the body that does a particular job, such as the heart or the stomach

planet

Huge round object that orbits a star

pollution

Waste that has been dumped in water, in the air, or on land. Pollution usually harms the environment

predator

Animal that lives by hunting and eating other animals

prey

Animal that is hunted for food

receptor

Part of the body that picks up information

satellite

Any object that moves around the Earth, often a human-made machine that collects scientific information

scuba

Equipment worn by divers that lets them breathe underwater

sensor

Part of a machine or robot that picks up information from the surroundings

space

Place beyond Earth's atmosphere

space probe

Unmanned spacecraft designed to study objects in space and send information back to the Earth

star

Huge glowing ball of gas

submarine

Boat that can sail on top of the sea or dive deep underwater

telescope

Instrument used to look at distant objects

turbine

Wheel or rotor that is turned to make power, used in places such as wind farms

webcam

A camera that sends photographs or images over the Internet

Index

Acknowledgements

DK would like to thank the following: Dave Ball and Katie Knutton for design assistance; Yamini Panwar for hi-res co-ordination; Caroline Hunt for proofreading; and Helen Peters for the index.

The publisher would like to thank the following for their kind permission to reproduce their photographs:

(Key: a-above; b-below/bottom; c-centre; f-far; l-left; r-right; t-top)

1 123RF.com: Andrzej Tokarski / ajt (clb); Mariusz Blach (crb); Imagehit Limited | Exclusive Contributor (cb). **Alamy Stock Photo:** Samyak Kaninde (br). **Dorling Kindersley:** Wildlife Heritage Foundation, Kent, UK (crb/Leopard). **Dreamstime.com:** Diosmirnov (c); Shakila Malavige; Santos06 (bl); Okea (crb/Coffee); Dragoneye (bc). **Fotolia:** Auris (cla). 2-3 Dreamstime.com: Shakila Malavige. 4-5 Dreamstime.com: Shakila Malavige. 4 Dreamstime.com: Tuulijumala (br). 5 Dreamstime.com: Jaroslaw Grudzinski / jarek78 (bc, br). 6-7 Dreamstime.com: Shakila Malavige. 8 Alamy Stock Photo: Granger Historical Picture Archive (clb). 8-9 NASA: ESA; G. Illingworth, D. Magee, and P. Oesch, University of California, Santa Cruz; R. Bouwens, Leiden University; and the HUDF09 Team. 9 NASA: (ca). 10-11 Dreamstime.com: Shakila Malavige. 11 NASA: JPL-Caltech (ca). PunchStock: Westend61 / Rainer Dittrich (cla). 12-13 Dreamstime.com: Shakila Malavige. 13 NASA: Carla Thomas (tr). 14-15 Dreamstime.com: Shakila Malavige. 15 Dreamstime.com: Jacglad (clb). NASA: MPIA / Calar Alto Observatory (br). 16 Dreamstime.com: Clearviewstock (crb); Lars Christensen / C-foto (bc). 16-17 Dreamstime.com: Shakila Malavige. 17 Dorling Kindersley: Andy Crawford (tr). 18 123RF.com: Boris Stromar / astrobobo. **Dreamstime.com:** Loren File / Lffile (Flag). 18-19 Dreamstime.com: Shakila Malavige. 19 NASA: (c). 20 123RF.com: luisrsphoto (bl). **Dreamstime.com:** Melonstone (crb). 20-21 Dreamstime.com: Shakila Malavige. 21 123RF.com: Andrzej Tokarski / ajt (cla); klotz (crb); Vitalii Artiushenko (ca). **Dreamstime.com:** Terracestudio (ca/Hat). 22 123RF.com: Imagehit Limited | Exclusive Contributor (cb); Pongsak Polbubpha (cl); Mariusz Blach (cb/Coffee cup). **Dreamstime.com:** Okea (br); Shakila Malavige (t). 23 123RF.com: Mariusz Blach (clb). **Dreamstime.com:** Bigphoto (cb); Grafner (cr). 24-25 Dreamstime.com: Shakila Malavige. 24 123RF.com: Gino Santa Maria / ginosphotos (cr); lurin (cb). **Dreamstime.com:** Mangojuicy (bl). 25 123RF.com: Andrew Barker (cb); Stanislav Pepeliaev (bl); mreco99 (tl). **Getty Images:** Erik Simonsen (t). 26 Alamy Stock Photo: Hideo Kurihara (cra). **U.S. Geological Survey:** (b). 26-27 Dreamstime.com: Shakila Malavige. 27 Dorling Kindersley: Stephen Oliver (cr). **US Geological Survey:** 28 123RF.com: Александр Ермолаев / Ermolaev Alexandr Alexandrovich / photodeti (ca). **Alamy Stock Photo:** Benny Marty (cl). **Dorling Kindersley:** Jerry Young (ftl, tc). 29 Dorling Kindersley: Gyuri Csoka Cyorgy (fcr). **Dreamstime.com:** Cosmin Manci / Cosmin (cr); Johnfoto (tl). 30-31 Dreamstime.com: Shakila Malavige. 30 Dreamstime.com: Alisali (c). 31 123RF.com: ccat82 (crb). **Dreamstime.com:** Alle (clb, c). iStockphoto.com: thawats (cl). 32 Dreamstime.com: Christophe Testi (c); Travelling-light (c/Pad). 32-33 Dreamstime.com: Shakila Malavige. 33 Dreamstime.com: Guido Nardacci (cr). 34 Dreamstime.com: Iakov Filimonov / Jackf (cl). **Getty Images:** Rhinie van Meurs / NIS / Minden Pictures (cr). 34-35 Dreamstime.com: Shakila Malavige. 35 Dreamstime.com: Jlcst (br); Travelling-light (cb). 36 123RF.com: Steve Byland (clb). **Alamy Stock Photo:** B Christopher (cb). 37 123RF.com: Ten Theeralerttham / rawangtak (cl, fcra). **Alamy Stock Photo:** blickwinkel (c); imageBROKER (cra); Roberto Nistri (fcl, cr); Samyak Kaninde (br). **Dorling Kindersley:** Wildlife Heritage Foundation, Kent, UK (cb). **Dreamstime.com:** Dragoneye (bl); Kevin Panizza / Kpanizza (ca); Fenkie Sumolang / Fenkieandreas (tr). **Getty Images:** Paul Kay (c/Green sponge). 38-39 Dreamstime.com: Shakila Malavige. 38 Dorling Kindersley: Thomas Marent (cr). **Fotolia:** Eric Isselee (c). 39 Alamy Stock Photo: Amazon-Images (bc); Life on White (br). **Dorling Kindersley:** Jerry Young (crb, bl); Natural History Museum, London (cla/Butterfly); Andrew Beckett (Illustration Ltd) (cl). **Dreamstime.com:** Travelling-light (cla). **Getty Images:** Gravity Images (cla). 40 123RF.com: Ekasit Wangprasert (cl); rawpixel (crb). **Dreamstime.com:** ArchitectureVIZ (clb); Whilerests (cb); Haiyin (fcl); Maksim Toome / Mtoome (c). 40-41 Dreamstime.com: Shakila Malavige. 41 123RF.com: Andrey Kryuchkov / varunalight (c); jezper (cb). **Dreamstime.com:** Radha Karuppannan / Radhuvenki (cla); Jan Martin Will (br). **Getty Images:** Jeff J Mitchell / Staff (crb); Miles Willis / Stringer (ca). 42-43 Dreamstime.com: Shakila Malavige. Science Photo Library: Steve Gscmeissner (c/Dust mite). 42 Dreamstime.com: Sebastian Kaulitzki / Eraxion (cb). **Science Photo Library:** Steve Gscmeissner (c). 43 Getty Images: Kateryna Kon / Science Photo Library (clb); Science Photo Library (b). 44-45 123RF.com: Natallia Yeumenenka (cb). 45 Depositphotos Inc: chaoss (ca). **Dreamstime.com:** Alexey Romanenko

/ Romanenkoalexey (bc). 46-47 Dreamstime.com: Shakila Malavige. 47 Dreamstime.com: Tuulijumala (cra). 48-49 Dreamstime.com: Shakila Malavige. 48 123RF.com: Peter Lewis (c). **Dreamstime.com:** Bjørn Hovdal (cra). 49 123RF.com: Evgeny Atamanenko (ca); Peter Lewis (cl). **Dreamstime.com:** Cebas1 (cra). 50-51 Dreamstime.com: Shakila Malavige. 50 123RF.com: Aleksandr Belugin (cra); Andriy Popov (clb). **Dreamstime.com:** Petr Jilek (clb/Mud). 51 Dreamstime.com: Daniel Ryan Burch (ca); Petr Jilek (bc). 52-53 Dreamstime.com: Shakila Malavige. 52 123RF.com: Dejan Lazarevic (r). **Dorling Kindersley:** A. Hardesty (cl). 53 Dreamstime.com: Daniela Pelazza (clb); Jannoon028 (clb/wood); Santos06 (cb). **Getty Images:** Andrew Harrer / Bloomberg (cb/Object). 54-55 Dreamstime.com: Shakila Malavige. 54 Dreamstime.com: Lars Christensen / C-foto (cra). 55 123RF.com: belchonock (clb/Clock); yarruta (cla); Tim Markley (bc). **Depositphotos Inc:** tangjans (clb). **Dreamstime.com:** Georgii Dolgykh (ca); Marilyn Gould (cl); Vladvitek (cr). 56-57 Dreamstime.com: Shakila Malavige. 56 123RF.com: tobi (cl). **Dreamstime.com:** Diosmirnov (ca); Winai Tepsuttinun (r). 57 Dreamstime.com: Diosmirnov (c); Travelling-light (cla). 58 Dorling Kindersley: Jerry Young (c, crb/Snail). **Dreamstime.com:** Brad Calkins (crb); Travelling-light (bc); Elena Schweitzer / Egal (cra); Olga Popova / Popovaphoto (cra/Marker); Jannekespr (bl). 58-59 Dreamstime.com: Shakila Malavige. 59 123RF.com: Andrzej Tokarski / ajt (cb). **Dorling Kindersley:** Booth Museum of Natural History, Brighton (ca, ftr). **Dreamstime.com:** Andrey Burmakin / Andreyuu (c/Shield bug); Svetlana Larina / Blair_witch (ca/Butterfly, ftr/Butterfly); Cosmin Manci / Cosmin (ca/Beetle, c/Beetle); Isselee (ca/Firebug, c/Firebug); Sutisa Kangvansap / Mathisa (cl, cr). **Fotolia:** Auris (ca/Flask). 60 123RF.com: Natthapon Ngamnithiporn (cb). 60-61 Dreamstime.com: Shakila Malavige. 61 123RF.com: Steve Collender (cr); Antonio Balaguer Soler (fcr). **Dreamstime.com:** Minaret2010 (bc). 62 Alamy Stock Photo: Maurice Savage (c); Mihai Andritoiu - Creative (cb); oroch (br). 62-63 Alamy Stock Photo: Arch White (t). **Dreamstime.com:** Shakila Malavige. 63 Alamy Stock Photo: Clair Dunn (ca); Xinxin Cheng (c); Mark Davidson (crb). **Dreamstime.com:** Shakila Malavige; Zhanghaobeibei (c). 64-65 Dreamstime.com: Shakila Malavige; Zhanghaobeibei (c). 64 Alamy Stock Photo: Granger Historical Picture Archive (crb). 65 123RF.com: spaxia (c). **Dorling Kindersley:** Stephen Oliver (cl). **Dreamstime.com:** Gv1961 (tr); Luis Louro (bc); Nadezhda1906 (br). 66 Alamy Stock Photo: Dariusz Kuzminski (tl); studiomode (cra). 66-67 Dreamstime.com: Shakila Malavige. 67 Dorling Kindersley: Fleet Air Arm Museum (c, bc). **Dreamstime.com:** Chris Brignell (fcra, cra). 68-69 Dreamstime.com: Shakila Malavige. 69 Dreamstime.com: Maksym Gorpenyuk / Tass (cra); Yudesign (tl). 70-71 Dreamstime.com: Shakila Malavige. 70 123RF.com: Pablo Scapinachis Armstrong (bc). **Dreamstime.com:** Kitchner Bain (bc/TV). 71 123RF.com: Kanoksak Tameeraksa (cla). **Dreamstime.com:** Dary423 (cr); Juan Moyano (cra); Milkos (crb). 72 Dreamstime.com: Ali Mustafa Pişkin (cra); Tuulijumala (cl); Axstokes (clb, crb); Erol Berberovic (cb). **iStockphoto.com:** Luca di Filippo (cr). 72-73 Dreamstime.com: Shakila Malavige. 73 Dorling Kindersley: Peter Minister (cra/T.Rex). **Dreamstime.com:** Ali Mustafa Pişkin (tl); Robwilson39 (tc); Angelo Gilardelli (cra); Profyart (cr); Badboo (crb); Axstokes (fcrb). **Fotolia:** Maxim Kazmin (tl/Computer). 74-75 Dreamstime.com: Shakila Malavige. 74 123RF.com: Kanoksak Tameeraksa (ca). **Dorling Kindersley:** John Rigg, The Robot Hut (clb). **Getty Images:** John B. Carnett / Bonnier Corporation (bc). **Humanoid robot created by Softbank Robotics** (cra). 75 123RF.com: chris brignell (cb); goodluz (cra); Thomas Hecker (clb, cb/Frame); Vadym Andrushchenko (fcrb). **Dreamstime.com:** Alex Scott / Alexjpscott (clb/Garden); Nikolai Sorokin (crb). **iStockphoto.com:** ernie decker (tc). **Knightscope, Inc.:** (bl). 76 Alamy Stock Photo: Roberto Nistri (bc). **Dreamstime.com:** Kevin Panizza / Kpanizza (br). 76-77 Dreamstime.com: Shakila Malavige. 77 NASA: JPL-Caltech (tc). 78-79 Dreamstime.com: Shakila Malavige. 80 Dreamstime.com: Shakila Malavige Endpaper images: *Front:* Dreamstime.com: Shakila Malavige; *Back:* Dreamstime.com: Shakila Malavige.

Cover images: *Front and Back:* Dreamstime.com: Diosmirnov (chef hats); *Front:* 123RF.com: alisali cl/ (flowers), Andrzej Tokarski / ajt crb/ (snail), Mariusz Blach br/ (cup), tobi tr/ (pot); **Alamy Stock Photo:** Samyak Kaninde bl/ (pika); **Dorling Kindersley:** Booth Museum of Natural History, Brighton cra/ (beetle), Wildlife Heritage Foundation, Kent, UK bl/ (leopard); **Dreamstime.com:** Alle fcl/ (bees), Andrey Burmakin / Andreyuu cra/ (bug), Cosmin Manci / Cosmin cr/ (beetle), Torian Dixon / Mrincredible tl/ (planets), Dragoneye bl/ (goat), Isselee cra/ (firebug), Okea br/ (coffee splash), Santos06 bc/ (cart), Shakila Malavige br/ (background), Sutisa Kangvansap / Mathisa cr/ (butterfly), Svetlana Larina / Blair_witch fclb/ (butterfly), Travelling-light tr/ (note pad); **NASA:** cla/ (Voyager); *Back:* 123RF.com: tobi cra/ (pot); **Dreamstime.com:** Jannoon028 crb/ (plank), Tommy Schultz / Tommyschultz clb/ (coral); **iStockphoto.com:** thawats fclb/ (butterfly); *Spine:* 123RF.com: goodluz b/ (remote control).

All other images © Dorling Kindersley
For further information see: www.dkimages.com